Tracing Ghosts

Poetry and fiction by
Cal Louise Phoenix

Kansas City　Spartan Press　Missouri

Spartan Press
Kansas City, Missouri
spartanpresskc.com

Copyright (c) Cal Louise Phoenix
First Edition 1 3 5 7 9 10 8 6 4 2
ISBN: 978-1-946642-67-7
LCCN: 2018953736

Design, edits and layout: Jason Ryberg
Cover image and author photo: Jeff Blank Photography
All rights reserved. No part of this publication may be reproduced or transmitted in any form or by any means, electronic or mechanical, including photocopying, recording or by info retrieval system, without prior written permission from the author.

Spartan Press would like to thank Prospero's Books, The Fellowship of N-finite Jest, The Prospero Institute of Disquieted P/o/e/t/i/c/s, Will Leathem, Tom Wayne, Jeanette Powers, j. d. tulloch, Jon Bidwell, Jason Preu, Mark McClane, Tony Hayden and the whole Osage Arts Community.

The author gratefully acknowledges the editors of the following publications where versions of these poems first appeared:

Burningword, fall 2011, issue 60: "Hard Times,"
seveneightfive, fall 2012, volume four, issue eight: "Keystone House,"
Inscape, spring 2013, issue 38: "Balcony" and "Two Bed, Two Bath,"
FLARE: the Flagler Review, fall 2013, volume 24, issue one: "Overcast,"
Apeiron Review, winter 2014, issue eight: "Ophidiophobia,"
Scapegoat Review, winter 2014, issue 16: "Ode to Slight,"
Cactus Heart, summer 2015, issue twelve: "Once a Month Reminder,"
30 N, spring 2016 edition: "May 31st,"
Sink Hollow, spring 2016, volume one: "A Weekend, One April,"
Green Blotter, spring 2016 edition, "Note of Apology,"
Welter, spring 2016 edition, "Roommates,"
pamplemousse, volume 4, issue 1, "The Farmhouse,"
Lindenwood Review, spring 2017, issue seven, "Casual(ties)"

CONTENTS

May 31st / 1

Ophidiophobia / 3

Hard Times / 5

Balcony / 7

Two Bed, Two Bath / 9

Overcast / 11

Keystone House / 12

Once a Month Reminder / 14

A Weekend, One April / 15

Ode to Slight / 16

Note of Apology / 17

Roommates / 19

Casual(ties) / 21

In Brooklyn / 23

Soulmate / 25

Spies Unto Themselves / 26

Lost Scarf / 27

A Refreshing Change of Pace / 28

After Seven O'clock / 30

Cognitive Fumbling / 32

Relics / 34

Setting Boundaries / 36

The Farmhouse / 39

To Alex, Kamyar, and Bevel,
who have refused to disappear.

May 31st

Tulips are not my favored flowers,
but I would have been married
in a garden of their bulbs.
The dress was a polka dotted shock
exposing knobby limbs and unshaven legs
tipped with bare feet.

I would have sweat in the garden
until makeup and guests grew stale.
Until the decor and food
had congealed
and the parking lot was vacant.

My soulmate's costume was to be a jar
with a tarnished lid and green tie.
But, before he would fit our altar
he left me for a sofa
of secrets and whiskey breath.

I put on sneakers and wandered
old haunts for somewhere abandoned
to hang my lipstick sign.
Months passed, marked
by cardboard boxes and emptied bottles.

Spring brought the stink of neglected towels.
On that day, I prayed for rain—no dice.
Eyes were rolled by friends
who passed around sunscreen.

It will rain this autumn, and once it has
I'll bury my soulmate
among the grey lackluster of expired earth.
I'll take the jar home
and drink from it—a juice of tulip bulbs.
There will be no jacket and tie to burn.

Ophidiophobia

When it started, we were hummingbirds.
We played tragic
by comparing strange dreams and other head sounds.
We laughed at broken guitar strings
and stubbed coins.

In the rain, we canned ourselves in glass
and blew smoke through the cracks. In the heat,
we peeled away our foliage and sweat in watercolors
until all of the furniture was new.

We drew plans until they became mistakes,
but kept making love to the maps—even after
they had shriveled and fallen
from the face of the refrigerator.

Now, he weighs me into sofa foam
and plucks me with his tongue
to keep the words from blooming.
His calloused tips—and teeth too—
cut my backside into decorative scales:
red to blue to yellow—all slick, all swollen.

Once my limbs, my keys and earrings
are lost in the tumble, I slither gone
to sleep in the dark beneath the soft house of his liver.
While he quiets in the hum of an amber cloud,
I wish for another warm summer.

Hard Times

"In hard times, beauty can seem frivolous—but take it away
and all you're left with is hard times."

–Paul Madonna, *Everything is Its Own Reward*

grey matter mush, a heart attack
the older brother died at thirty-one
the younger one was picked up put away
his underpaid lawyer tired smiled patted shoulders
fifteen more months of under-seasoned 'meat'
—could be worse

salt water halo
I leave the door ajar while I sort refold repack
the sweaters shirts jeans shorts
tags still attached until he gets back
a scavenger, I eat on food stamps and dig myself
a sanctuary
in a compiled dust old junk grease stains house
spiders watch me shower

my saintly lover sighs, and I apologize
we met at the start of shit falling apart
our summers bring bad drivers sweat cat hair
everywhere
so, we take to the mountains
escaping the stink and thinking

for a week, climbing soggy cheese and trail mix
watching the kaleidoscope landscape
crumble into night
he holds me steady, and I can breathe

Balcony

my lion boy and I were crouching embracing
on the balcony
following the speed of the metropolis swept night
country dame, I was stunned not to see stars, yet
felt terribly small

just two pale lumps
pressed against the bars boards balancing
on palms and the balls of our feet
while dog walkers and sleazes zig-zagged
the street below
unaware, as we were unknowing
to our own glowing guts

forced to pace ourselves by the matters
alive within our homes
I stole looks into his obsidian eyes
while the chilly breezes prickled our near naked limbs

we were strangers made soul mates inside
an airport terminal
after endless stacks of postcards
and late-night long-distance calls

—years since, I still smell him in my skin
and nuzzle the dark for his phantom
even though the rotation of this rock has
crushed our loving heads into corruption,
the pining still glimmers
in spite of becoming unfamiliar once again

Two Bed, Two Bath

the fog was coast-low when I arrived
with more luggage in head than hands
distrust a glue fastening my lips
your eyes kept me still
above our tinkling glasses in your new house

its wind-shifted bedroom walls whispered amongst
the bed where I laid alone fully clothed
limbs peeking forth to cradle
books papers television remote
I couldn't warm myself while the cold lived deep
in my bones

for hours, my feet traced the creaking hardwood
cautiously fingering the edges of hand towels
inspecting the guts of shelves
staring through frosted windows prodded by
ice slicked branches
the quiet was loud, so I talked at the cat who too
eyed me suspiciously
twelve hours bereft and later still, even after
your movements woke the rooms
the volume of your justifying sent me into the hallway
upstairs bathroom twisting the tap splashing water
onto my brow my neck

I was still hunched over shaky
breathing into my cupped hands
when I returned to configure the next move
in the numb map
of your unexpectedly strange face

Overcast

a calendar means to pine by every square
—those aching seasons float by on notes of old words
for a year, *I think my brain might fall out*

the farmhouse has settled into disrepair:
dust veils the poetry scrawled walls my cookware
weeds have eaten our garden—those crops
abandoned to rot

and yet, upstairs I stay
sitting on the master bed
plucking webs as they collect from my eyelashes

and wear our fantasy like a shadow
though it bleeds to ripple my draperies
with a sticky shame that
keep my wrists and tongue in captivity

Keystone House
For Gavin...

"You must be somewhere in London, you must be loving your life in the rain." –The National, "England"

you don't know that you pulled me angsty shaking
out of a bathroom stall at The Tate,
clutching a purse of postcards
navigating hallways of rooms to mine,
the beer your voice made me dizzy

our lunch date became a clock to coordinate
I read and anxiously wandered about the hostel
not quite desperate American loud mouth,
I was glad when you kissed me
it made evening repacking more manageable

in your talk, I saw the Thai women holding umbrellas
against the sun,
the retired boxer with missing teeth
leading you to tango,
and I relished your Gaelic
—my mother's ancestral tongue

after picking up the flesh salt of contours,
quiet hands cupped
as we curved together for five hours of night
on a springy mattress with the trains grumbling
underground

in the morning, spilled coffee scorched
your dishwasher's knuckles
and when you accidently
stole my bag back with you,
the Piccadilly liners then witnessed
a wide-eyed bird-girl soar escalators

across the pond, I fell to blankets with strange air
and finally came out of the day-length love spell

there had been time enough for just a taste,
leaving me honey-mouthed
with bees trapped in my chest,
and reoccurring nights where I find you in my sleep

Once a Month Reminder

My uterus is a soured onion
spilling into a ceramic ash tray
casted the color of robes
and mended by whispy gold glue
of a whispy golden girl.

At two years, the lass could repair faults
without touching the tip
of the brush to her lips. So smart.

For nine months, I opened my entrails
to embrace her—a bunny in a bed.
There, we ate yogurt
and watched cartoons about candy

until I lost her inside a cardboard box
and was sacked for my troubles.

But no one goes forgotten by
a toddler in an endless tossing.

In my sleep, she still unearths
the onion from its dish and strokes it
into a vermillion gleam.
In my sleep, we share the imagination of
her father—a caricature who is afraid of blood.

A Weekend, One April

Straddling a worry doll,
I've fountained into a million reflective pieces.
It's the same feeling of being beside the sea
—of being buried.

One can retrace
having put my hands in the curly thicket of your hair
and licked its pastry scent from my upper lip
—you pulled the endless river of mine
until we both unraveled into puddles.

You taught me that I'm allergic to
coffee cups with liquor kissed rims and that
life is packing into ill-fitted spaces. You taught me
how to brood.

By the anxious eyeing of a hotel's digital clock—paused
with a worry: *have we become codependent?*

For four nights, I was the blood of your lungs.
The rest was accidental—*harassment!*
Someone will relearn to love patches
of cold cotton; my money's on the lion-hearted.

Ode to Slight

The vermillion wires of my muscles are padded
by strange, yellow bedding.

Mostly, I want to melt myself down
and bake cupcakes with the run-off.
I would serve them to my friends, watch them eat,
and want for nothing. Except to feel like rain.

Sometimes, I actually hug handfuls
of that weird laundry
and hack them into steaks. I am reminded
of how hungry I am,
but what looks like meat in the pan
springs pale shoots over the fire.

Note of Apology
For p.e. garcia...

Seasons expire—it's the price of
gleaning ties.

Urgently, dissolve to stained glass.
This is Chicago. This is Little Rock.
This is Kansas City.

It becomes a song
in our sides: *This is art now.*

A story about bees.
Something torn, like lace.
We bore it in dresses of translucent segments
and held each other
with throat-probing bloodletting fingers—two
sinking ships trading lifeboats.

One loves to shame, to paint
enemies of used condoms and hotel bills.

It won't end while
distance sketches the insufferable sting
of summer, while I wear
your shadow to bed.

Transitioning
praising grey—the lake became a vehicle
moving on, becoming fast

in forms that stretch into a comic darkness
and creep over yellowed grass and street debris.

You say your teeth don't remember—mine can't forget.

Roommates

If my body were a house,
my liver would be my soulmate.
I can always find him
behind the soft cream of my side
like a panting, bloated fruit.
I quell him with fire water and pastries
when my brain aches with clouds.
Which, it often does—at least two hours per day.

We keep my heart in its own closet
in the attic. Otherwise, my spine
curls into my knees with her weight.
I tried once to part the walls
of ribs for more roaming space.
But, she leapt out and took for the pinkish fog of
a streetlight down the block.

During her absence, my liver moved into her room.
I wrapped my arms to cup my back
to make time for him. My savings dried up. I stopped
brushing my teeth. The rooms crawled with musk.

Later, we found my heart huddled in litter,
beside a rusted dumpster. It took years
to pick the jaded stubble from her slick,
pounding surface.

She had never been one to act like that before
—nor had my soulmate been a catalyst for disease.
Maybe this spring, I'll hull them out
and let them soak in peppermint tea. I'll line the meat
with lemon peels before I put them back to bed.

Casual(ties)

For Huascar...

The cold descended before we bundled up
to tease storms without eyes.
You in your sweaters—me, of black and white movies.
There was soup and sex beside the prairie, gashed
by a highway where I eventually caved.

Defect was that you never understood
my need to ramble, my campfire wetness
—the suppression
of my echoing lungs. These little fits
keep me organized—it's the only way
that I can invite the Sandman into my bed.

Of course, books are built up as barricades
broken streets and fragmented lyrics are spun
by my frost-caught car, my hair dancing
in the window slit.

>At work, at the bar:
>*I swear that I'm not always like this.*

For thirty days, I was your fanciful art
hardening in those short solitary walks
to the apartment, from the parking lot
baring a nightgown of your cologne
—nevermind my toothbrush beside your straight razor
on the bathroom sink.

    At home, at work
     —filling myself with poetry in places
    where your fingers had kept me company.

It was a dull realization: when the wine runs out
we're still the same—two wolfish children
reared by mountainous escape towers
    two milky-skinned bunnies
    tearing scattered paths along those ridges.

When you finally wedged a lady red herring
into my locker and allowed it to act as a bandage
where you'd left me dented—*that was someone else,
I think*—relief lifted me
more than the wash of a squall ever could, more than
the fat pull at the finish of a glass.

In Brooklyn

we took the train to Brooklyn in the dark
while still drunk and falling
into the grim and grit sidewalk
off the street into the chained fences trash bins
I threw you
hands claws against your chest
and later, in the tunnels
my teeth too

with insides moaning please *please please take me*
head whirling
a raccoon and a couple of fat rats
skittered across our path
and you talked and talked—some nonsense
mouth words pursed like glitter

a guitar player playing jive
had strummed our subway stop, offering
some awful love song for cash
only then did you kiss me back—there, underground
tongue in my neck my palm cupping cock
until Long Island slid beneath our feet
and you wised up resisted
sent me backward in an airplane

once sober, I blamed a folk ideal in mind
I unpacked back to work, back to school

aching swollen apple-lipped
at last, the antics dissolved into a bitter mass
I couldn't swallow
but for two more years

Soulmate

bones are deceitful
lights tilting
to draw from all of the wrong corners

his tongue and eyes too—speckled eggs
resting in rippling flesh

I like to watch them as he plunges, as if he
means to break me with my own heart

there are streaks of honey where the dress pressed
where his mouth cut the expensive cloth
my mother helped to pick it out—she paid for it
to develop dust in a box beneath a box
beneath the smell of rain

I know him in my bones
as well as I know my bones exist at all
as well as I know the depth of blood's color

Spies Unto Themselves

hands prickle with clammy, would be smearing
sinew cracking beneath the posed weight
of public sight
expand to relax the cords of the neck
face staunch, potato starched—doom adaptive

the reinvention of old sketches, they become
pregnant with tension
he carries her knees
and she, the fleshy pieces beneath his thumbs

like a juice stained stubborn fabric wad
—it's pulse is a madness, a mark, a glad reminder

to follow this glimmer
into the hallowed, into the bunker
where the alarm hangs above their hats

kissing to protest the pull of twilight
prayers to ease the nervous mountain in their bellies

if the dam were, it would stand to be patched
until it appears: opened, parted
a quilt of private gestures

Lost Scarf

springtime in Chicago, she meets a man-child
of her time and mind, running like water

flowing over and beyond cupped palms
to stain the ground in candy-tones
those she sought after

    lapping up the ground
before a chance specter (a person of Porlock)
could press a shoe's mocking signature
into a moment that had lasted mere hours

choking on *adiós*, he lost a scarf
to the labyrinth coil of the 'L'
while she nicotine swam between cold sheets
and branded raccoon eyes, lips, and cheeks
into listless pillows which pretended to be

    that flower face, his bready smell
—a not quite hyperreal
assembled to complete
what had lacked the chance to start: fingers skimming
scars as sentences to be interrupted
at her slit and shadow
before splaying to grasp the warm dough
like a prize

A Refreshing Change of Pace
For Mark...

Like chocolate malt, he spills
into himself, his cotton sack of tree limbs.
Everything from the sweet curl of his spine
to his shirtless shoulders and razorblade hips
—his body is music, and she fumbles, pinched
and swollen, to keep up.

When she goes to him for sleep, he packs her tight
into musky sheets. The floor bites.
They use big words until dawn
claws at the slits in the drapes.
Sometimes, he says things that
> *when you look at me*
> *like that I feel*
> *so beautiful so beautiful when you*
> *make me come*

feel like guile, although he is a different, genuine sort
—exposed, white light on the inside. A healing balm.

Once, she pointed to his toe where there was blood
from a fresh scrape. He had not noticed, his senses
caught up elsewhere—her whirl? Her hair?

There is something about him that
intimidates her jaw. She is a quilt, and his voice
—dancing on observations and around complaints—
is a balloon in her bosom, a silver plume
a sliver of pressure. *I like how we fit together,* he says
and although she has drank
her coffee and gotten dressed
she won't wake up until he's gone.

After Seven O'clock

That summer sweltered as hot and wet
as the mouths they mashed together
to keep the wrong words from forming.
While he laid floors in cut-offs held up with rope
she listened to Mozart and collected butts
in failed ceramic projects.
The bent blinds and kneaded carpet whispered
of wanting—waiting until his truck belched
to a halt below the balcony.

Of parks and porches, they slapped bugs
scratched bites, and threw handfuls of sweat
from their brows and backs. In his shed, amongst
the smell of spoiled milk and cat piss, his knife-like hips
ground her mid-drift into cream.
After the humming had dissipated,
those bruises became welcomed company.

Before the string snapped (under breast, between ribs)
ten months unfolded. In the drunk cold, it happened:
>the calloused guitar cracking
>and carpenter's hand narrowed a finger
>from shelves to boxes, from the door
>to the trunk of her car.

When her feet began to drag, he carried her
back to bed for a final tumble
before putting her out on the porch like a stray,
where she surveyed the frost and grime
for a place to call *home.*

Growing up to ignore the spoon-shaking direction
of her father *(Watch out for those boys*
—the ones from the country) she gathers what she deserves:
> a backside of red and purple ribbons
> and the strain of an empty bottle,
> where she might have held her pride before.

Cognitive Fumbling

Once, I baked my brain
into a cake and pouted when it fell apart
after being turned onto the rack.
The mash was crumbled with feathers
and mixed with vodka. I set it on the counter to dry
inside the slit of light coming in through a gash
in the window. Hardened and cooled, I pushed
wheels into its corners and sent it out and away.

On a highway paved with black and white movies
and clementine rinds, it went.
The terrain was its own set: props of dried leaves,
salt, and black grit. At the end of the plot,
the little vehicle had come, gone
zipped along, picking up a patchwork
of reckless bruises finger-pressed prints
and the reek of deep regret
—something burnt and stale.

Returning, it carried secrets, borrowed
from pamphlets sketched by wagging tongues
and stern glances. Unrecognizable by then
I used it for a pillow until a future morning
when I'd grown tired of its lullaby
—a soundtrack of clichés in a vacuum:
groaning, weeping, self-pleading, and general agonizing.

Then, I took it back to the kitchen where I left it to boil
in a soup of rosemary, lemon, and dandelion root.
By dusk, all had evaporated
so I exchanged its place in my head with the pot instead.

Relics

For Bevel...

An ache is a petrol boost—not unlike
the weight of these cannons
resting where
our bones have molded into shipsides.

This boy and I had insides
on which we sailed: a swamp
of antique leaves and an alien's blue.
We drank each other from curly straws
swung matching mugs
and slurred from balcony points—it's the place

where we met and now visit
through a weak soup
a year and seven months too late.

We were meant to go ashore
on a postcard. It was done
once I comforted his belly with a drunk beetle

once he'd made me a believer
returning the favor underwater.

I discovered something holy then
in the third hour of the fifth morning
in the arch of my spine
in the writing in the sand—it's the place

where I've piled an altar
and now visit with tucked skirts
a year and five months too late.

Like a moth in horizon paints
he was swallowed by landscape.
My anchor was his request
the counter tilt of the wheel—transplanted
to a beach of dust and melted drywall.

Whisper-sung in an earthworm's breath
a clasp is my hymn:

Come, aim, boy. Light the fuse, boy. Hallelujah.

Setting Boundaries

One month, and we knew. That's why I hold you
here, five years later, at room's length
even when our bodies cup, our brains fuck
—too much remains unchanged.
>   Kissing was too intimate, you said.
>   I concealed the regrettable
>   shapes of my breasts, yet poured
>   the rest into your drinking glass
>   balanced on the disk
>   between dusk and twilight—you never
>   reciprocated, although I have seen you naked.

As you ate up my best, I spat glass. I inhaled frost.
In sum, loving you made me feel as small as a lentil.
That's why I hold you
here, presently, at sofa's length, at bed's length
at breath's length. Consumed without regard
—is that how it feels?
Do I turn your thoughts to marrow,
your bones to batter?

When the teasing begins to ache,
the blame is deflected
calling focus to the boozy insights,
the former purple river of my hair,

the parking lot expanse of my heart
—how these prompted your selection.
I think you idealized; you forget I've since repented

> —this many times scorned woman.
> Behold the product of imposed ego,
> the destruction internalized:
> the now me, a spidery figure in veils.
> Ravaged, I've sewn up my raped parts
> with quilting thread
> and become a frigid old cat.

Fend me off then, when the old hurt bubbles,
like Saintly George in polished armor,
charging the dragon, like garlic to a succubus.
Crush the younger version's head against the rocks.
Bury the spirits in the reek of herbs. Only when
you make soup should you recall the past
—because too much remains unchanged.

> This me, who you consider your siren,
> is not unique—a bit of flesh
> encapsulating a speck of intellect.
> While its design will carry musk and conversation,
> there's no room in these pockets
> for the hard stuff, the stuff below the pangs.

Pluck as you may, but my heartstrings go on for miles
circling decades, pinned to some places, and yes
maybe one spot bears a page, your brand scrawled there.

That's why I hold you
here today, at sigh's length,
even though your hands are too small
to hold the deeper parts, even if you have
the most beautiful feet of any man I've seen.
I would know; I still remember,
five years ago, watching you walk away.

The Farmhouse

For p.e. garcia and C. Hopkins...

The doorway braces to grip the man as he leans into it. His lover has finished dividing batter into the individual cups and now slides the tray into the tiny hell of the oven. Once the door is shut, he watches as she lowers herself to the floor and puts her forehead to the hot glass. He snubs his cigarette in a dish on the counter and slinks up behind her. She doesn't move when his fingers slip through her hair and curl around her face and part her mouth. He squeezes, and she invites the taste of blood.

"Love?" he asks.

"Sometimes," she says, "I can't breathe unless your breath is in the air."

When he has wiped his hands and retreated to the back of the house, she tends to the leftovers and leaves the dishes to soak.

Despite the warmth of the brief afternoon sun, her joints ache, so instead of touring the garden and talking to the spouts, she meanders upstairs to her sewing room and library. There's a pile of mending on the window seat and she lands beside it. A button slips out of the bundle and bounces onto the rug. She extends to retrieve it and studies its smooth, plastic edge before tossing it onto her desk.

By now, the hallway and rooms begin to gossip amongst themselves. She focuses through the window, where the trees at the edge of the property open for the stretch of a gravel driveway. Their branches have bloomed and she counts the silhouettes in the leaves until the man has come into her view.

He is carrying one of his guitars and smoking out of one corner of his mouth, while singing from the other. She cannot hear him. His song is one of long, backward secrets.

*

A ginkgo and a willow have found stages beside each other, planted by the previous residents. They stand in the front yard, just outside the crop lines. The day is warmed by a half-dressed sun, but the ginkgo is out of sorts.

"I don't appreciate your shadow," it tells the willow. "It smothers."

The willow doesn't reply, so the ginkgo clarifies: "Your shadow—it smothers. I'm being smothered by your shadow."

Still, the willow says nothing, but some of its leaves brown and detach into the wind.

*

The weight of the man's melancholy has forced him to
bed early. She tries to kiss and stroke him into sleep,
but he rolls away from her to melt into the fluff of the
overdressed mattress. Leaving him, she turns the lamp
off too soon and bangs her knee on the bedframe while
navigating the dark. Her cursing startles the hall, but the
door to the sewing room cracks with a soft squeal.

Inside, she limps passed the desk and wanders the spines
of her crowded bookcases. One wriggles a little, prompting
her to take it.

When she lifts the book to her lips, she finds that the pages
no longer smell of apple pastry. The discovery is a disappointment more terrible than waiting.

*

"You said once that we had the same eyes. Do you remember that?"

He smiles and drags an index along her chin. "Yeah," he says.

"I don't agree, actually," she says. "Your eyes are lighter than mine. They are like the English Channel, while mine look more like… Like the dark interior of some cavern."

*

Once in a while, she becomes bedridden for a day, bleeding postcards. Her flesh opens in slits to expel the hard paper. The pain is something supernatural.

The man waits on her, bringing her orange juice and decaffeinated tea. When she doesn't look, he collects the cards from the rug so that he can mediate on the images when he is alone and she is better.

His favorite bears a photo of a blonde toddler, standing near the center of a snow-laden parking lot. The backside reads, *They were right about you.* The message pokes at a queasy ache in his stomach, yet he cannot bring himself to get rid of it. Tucked into a notebook and pushed to the bottom of his sock drawer, it rests and he's never forgotten that it's there.

*

Spring is challenging the afternoon with a breeze like florescent graffiti when the phone rings. She quickly rinses the mashed bananas from her hands and wets the receiver as she picks up.

No voice accepts her greeting, but she understands.

"I need some way to tell you that I love you," she says before setting the receiver back into its cradle. Through the window, the man is returning from the shed with a rusty, grey tool box and an armful of short, white oak boards. His image shudders as it grows closer.

"It never ends," she murmurs, watching him gain vibrancy with every step.

✷

Finally, she put putty in the keyholes to keep the eyes of the hallways at bay.

✷

Lately, and only at night, she is filled with a curious desperation that she combats by sitting in the rocking chair on the porch. Sometimes, she only stays there long enough to smoke a cigarette. Other evenings, she'll fall asleep by the creaking of the chair.

Once, he asked about her routine: "Do you enjoy the company of the stars?"

"No," she said. "I would will them into polka-dots and wear the sky to my grave, if that were the case."

Her explanation filled him with an awful buzzing. Inside their shared bathroom, he wept into the sink and wished his face was that of someone else's.

Now, he knows when she has fallen asleep because the buzzing returns to rouse him. He sits up, pulls on a pair of thick socks, and descends to retrieve her. Cocooned to his chest, she continues to sleep, though her fingers still curl into the blush meat of his shoulders for balance.

*

The man is sitting at the kitchen table. His hair is dirty and he is wearing an extension cord for a belt. He pulls from a bottle of cheap rum and motions to her with the cap.

"But seriously, bell peppers are so fucking good; every other vegetable can kill itself."

She has prepared peppers stuffed with black beans, scrambled eggs, diced tomatoes, and yellow onion. The man's commentary gives her goosebumps, for pleasing others is how she best warms her bones.

"I'm going to make granola pancakes tomorrow. I thought raspberry jam would be great on top of them."

"That sounds fucking excellent."

In her giddiness, she neglects the hole in the corner of the oven mitt and moves to extract the baked peppers from the oven.

"Ballocks!" she cries, almost dropping the ceramic dish. The pad of her left ring finger becomes a white pucker.

While she cuddles the burn in her mouth, the man leans across the table, narrowing his eyes at her. "You know," he says, "I really hate the word *ballocks*."

She gapes at him, and her shame is like a cloak.

*

He has teased her so much about the existence of the Mothman that she's sometimes wary about driving at night. But when they've ran out of granulated garlic and soy milk, she forces herself to don a sweater and trace the darkness until she's been temporarily enveloped by the artificial lighting of the grocery store.

On her way back, she watches for awkward forms in the apexes of trees. Once parked, she bolts for the imaginary safety of the porch.

The pounded cries of the piano's keys welcome her before the front door is unlocked and pushed aside. Her companion is drunk and wears a thrifted mini-dress and stiletto boots. A brunette, polyester wigs sags to one side of his head. He has on hot pink lipstick and sunglasses with wide, square lens.

"Listen to this, tiny dancer!" he brays, still playing. "I've got something novel!"

She doesn't linger, opting to drop off her load in the kitchen. When the jagged music ends, he has followed her.

He takes her wrist from reaching for a mug and smears whiskey in kisses along her neck.

"Aw, what's up, kitten cat?" he clucks. "I danced around the living room while you were gone. I feel beautiful and unique tonight." He bites her, before adding, "Which is exactly what you are."

His hands have moved from tracing her hips to gripping them. His dress catches, exposing a twisted garter and a thickening bulge.

"Please stop," she says. "You know that you're too rough when you're drunk."

"Okay, sorry." He lets go. "Will you listen to my new song?"

"Sure. Let me put the kettle on first."

While the burner heats, she enters the hall to find the man lying on the rug.

"My head is too big for my body," he tells her.

She responds by lowering herself to the floor. She removes his wig and rubs his neck until the kettle prompts her to get up again. Then, she remains standing until it is time to go to bed.

*

"I took an early sleep. Dreamt that houses have relatives —you know—other certain houses. I was living in the brother of the house that I grew up in, the house that burned down. I sensed its sadness in the paint, in the apathetic kilter of the chimney. I became close with the house and secretly wished to be its brother. As I was walking up to it, fire suddenly erupted from all of the windows."

He pauses to steal a long drag from his cigarette and scratches a bite on his shin. She looks into and beyond the garden and digs her fingernail into the flaking paint of the porch swing. She is holding her breath.

"The fucking house wanted me to see it burn down," he says. "It fucking waited for me to come into view."

∗

Two cats sun themselves in grass that is soft and doesn't prickle. The caramel-colored long hair turns to the calico.

"What have we done?" it asks.

"We rushed," says the other, turning its head toward the ruddy, distant geography. Looking back, its companion has dissolved into the breeze. Its presence is replaced by the faraway cries of anonymous birds.

∗

Only the bed stays behind, dressed by her shadow. He can still smell her in the creases, in the tremors of his sleep.

Eventually, he moves his dresser to the living room. There, he rests on the sofa, pillowed by excuses, and falls asleep to the electric chirp of the television. It obscures the scraping of the bedframe as it drags across the hard wood –and the unanimous *shhh!* of the rug and window curtains who want her to stop.

*

Some years have passed when another house presents itself to the woman. It's yellow, with rooms that swing to encapsulate a slumping, winding stairwell. The walls are collages and its dusty carpet pulses with gentle music. There, she sleeps on the floor of a child's old bedroom. A different, delicate man's chest cradles the draperies of her arms and eyelashes. In the morning, he boils water for tiny cups of brazen coffee. As they smoke, they map symphonies from sentences. He makes her feel that nothing is objective.

When someone mentions commitment, they consider the scenario before agreeing swim in the rivers of each other instead. This suits her well enough for now –now that she has tired of the smell of crumbling glue and vintage wallpaper.

Cal Louise Phoenix was born, raised, and educated in Kansas, where she continues to reside. Her poetry, fiction, and nonfiction have appeared in literary publications since 2010, including her essay "Renovating Shabbat," which won the Beecher's 2015 Contest in nonfiction. *Tracing Ghosts* is her first book.

This project was made possible, in part, by generous support from the Osage Arts Community.

Osage Arts Community provides temporary time, space and support for the creation of new artistic works in a retreat format, serving creative people of all kinds — visual artists, composers, poets, fiction and nonfiction writers. Located on a 152-acre farm in an isolated rural mountainside setting in Central Missouri and bordered by ¾ of a mile of the Gasconade River, OAC provides residencies to those working alone, as well as welcoming collaborative teams, offering living space and workspace in a country environment to emerging and mid-career artists. For more information, visit us at www.osageac.org

Osage Arts Community

www.ingramcontent.com/pod-product-compliance
Lightning Source LLC
Chambersburg PA
CBHW030133100526
44591CB00009B/640